HOW TO PLAY

THE VIOLIN

A Beginner's Guide to Learning the Basics, Reading Music and Playing Songs with Audio Recordings

Legal & Disclaimer

The information contained in this book and its contents is not designed to replace or take the place of any form of medical or professional advice; and is not meant to replace the need for independent medical, financial, legal or other professional advice or services, as may be required. The content and information in this book has been provided for educational and entertainment purposes only.

The content and information contained in this book has been compiled from sources deemed reliable, and it is accurate to the best of the Author's knowledge, information, and belief. However, the Author cannot guarantee its accuracy and validity and cannot be held liable for any errors and/or omissions. Further, changes are periodically made to this book as and when needed.

Where appropriate and/or necessary, you must consult a professional (including but not limited to your doctor,

Table of Contents

Throughout this book there are musical examples and audio recordings to follow along with on your journey to learn how to play the violin.

Whenever you see the following outline:

Listening Example: Exercise 1

Please follow along with the recordings at the Sound Cloud link below or search on Sound Cloud for "How to Play the Violin".

https://soundcloud.com/jason_randall/sets/how-to-play-the-violin

Chapter 1

Introduction

Welcome to the beginner's guide to the violin! Congratulations on your decision to learn how to play. The violin is unique, interesting and easy to learn. It appears as a part of big orchestras, as a solo instrument, and in various kinds of non-classical music including blues, country, and rock. This book will teach you how to make your first sounds and develop a solid musical foundation for your future musical endeavors.

A Brief History of the Violin

The roots and development of the violin are hard to establish with certainty; however, today we can distinguish two basic lines. The first originates from Asia. An ancient Indian instrument called the ravanahatha involved the use of a bow and strings before it was known in Europe.

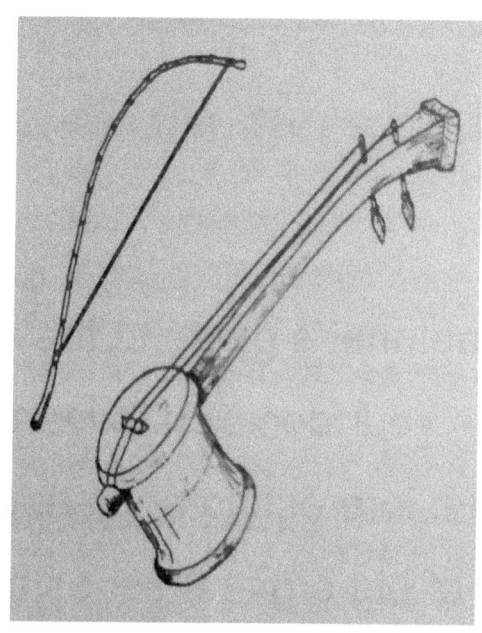

Pic.1 Ravanahatha

Arabic instruments called the rebab and the kemanche are the mediators between the ravanahatha and the first European versions of the violin. From the 8th century, when the Moors occupied the Iberian Peninsula, we can see the development of string instruments with a bow and a pear-shaped body, like the rebec or gigue.

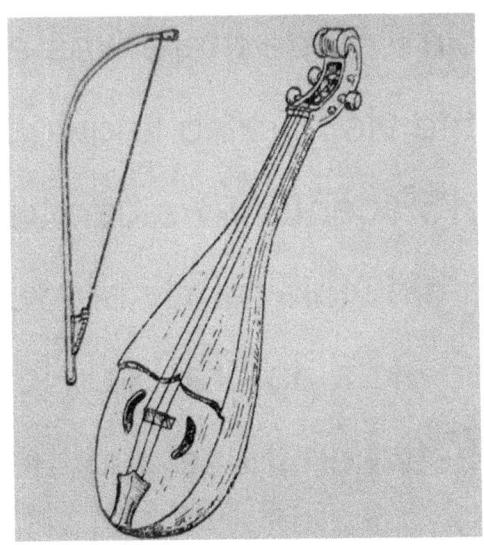

Pic.2 Rebec

The Second line originates from the instruments of the ancient Greeks; more precisely from their cithara — one of the oldest string instruments.

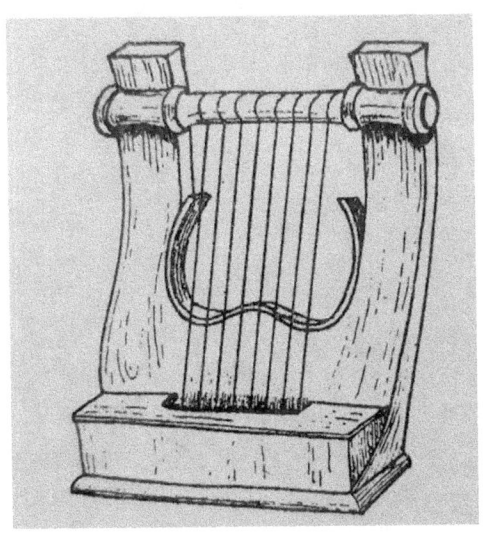

Pic.3 Cithara

In the 10th century in France there was a popular instrument called the vielle (also known as fidel or vioula), and by the end of 15th century we can track the development of an old viola family of two different types: viola da gamba and viola da braccio. However, there are many differences between these and the contemporary violin.

Finally, we have the lira da braccio, which is considered the immediate predecessor of the modern violin and viola.

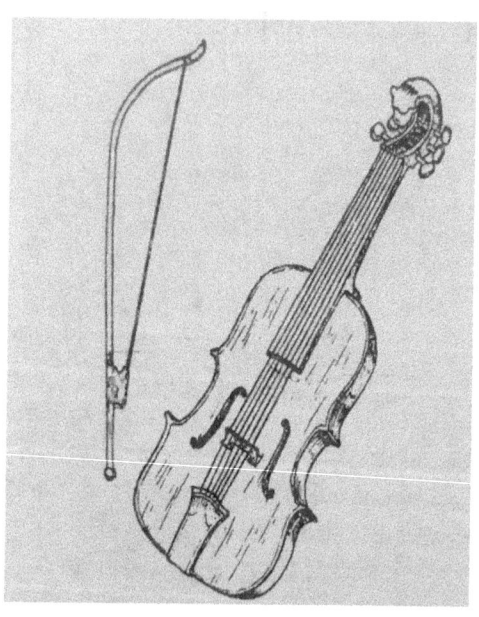

Pic.4 Lira da braccio

The cradle of the modern violin's development was two small towns in Northern Italy called Brescia and Cremona. They are also known for producing the most perfect, expensive and unsurpassed violins. Most prominent violin builders come from two families in Cremona: Amati and Guarneri.

Andrea Amati (1510-1586) was the founder of the Cremona school of violin and is credited with making the first violin family instruments that are used today. His grandson Niccoló Amati (1596-1684) was a builder and teacher of other violin masters. His most famous students were Andrea Guarneri (1626-1698) and the most famous of them all, Antonio Stradivari (1644-1737), whose instruments represent the peak of violin construction, both in sonority and harmony. There are, of course, other prominent schools in Germany, France, England, Netherlands, Czech Republic and others, but Italy has occupied first place to this day.

As for bow development, the first two in the picture below have an origin of hunting or warrior arches. The third was used in the 15th century and the fourth in the 17th century. Arcangelo Corelli (1653-1713), Giuseppe Tartini (1692-1770), Wilhelm Cramer (1745-1799) and Giovanni Battista Viotti (1753-1824) have led the bow to its current design (the last four bows in the picture below).

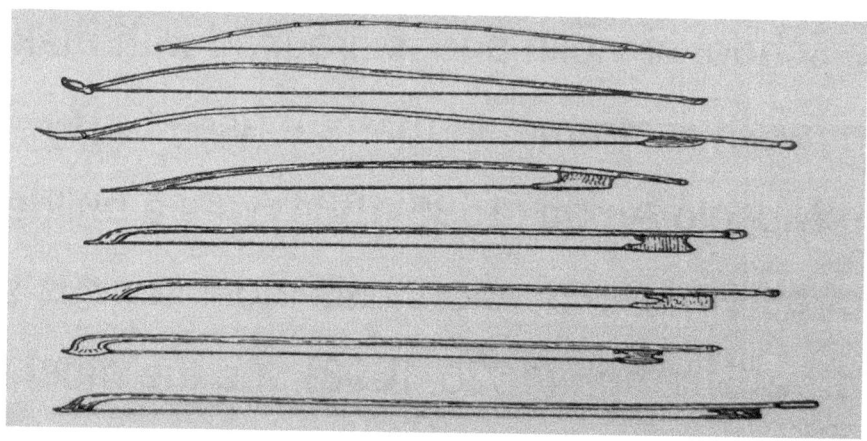

Pic.5 Bow development

Chapter 2

The Violin Parts, Tuning, and General Care

Topics Covered:

- Parts of the violin

- How to prepare your violin for practice

- How sound is produced

- Tuning

- Basic care

After buying your violin, it may seem ready to use, but looks can be deceiving! The violin has many parts we must know about if we want to properly control this beautiful instrument. In this chapter you will learn how to manage your violin from the moment you open your case to the moment you put it back in to rest until your next practice. You will know which parts of the violin are the most important to prepare for practice, how to tune your instrument, how to produce sound and how to treat your instrument when you're finished with practice.

Parts of the violin

The main part of the violin consists of its **body** (36 cm long), which has the role of a resonator. The front surface **(g)** is a bit convex and it can be made from various kinds of wood, but is usually made from spruce. The bottom surface **(h)** is made of maple. The brim of the violin consists of six curved slats and mostly determines the shape of the instrument. Inside the body we can see imported pieces of wood **(p, r, s)** which are there to put up with the additional pressure.

The **Neck** (24 cm long) **(e)** is fixed to the body and it has a **fingerboard (d)** on its front surface, which is usually made of ebony. At the upper end we have a **pegbox (o)**, which has four holes (two on each side) **(q)** in which we have four **tuning pegs.** At the top of the neck we can see the **scroll (a)**. The transition between the pegbox and the neck consists of the **nut (c)** — a small threshold which holds the **strings (f)**. Strings are stretched from pins along the neck and pass the **bridge (j),** where they reach their highest peak, and down to the **tailpiece (l),** which is a sort of string holder. On the upper part of the tailpiece we can find four tiny slots through which we pull the strings and where we can find the **fine tuners**. At the bottom of the tailpiece we can find the **end pin (n),** and finally we have the **chinrest (m)**.

Pic.6 Violin – front, back and opened

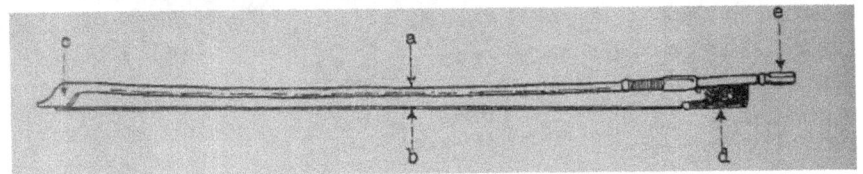

Pic.7 Violin bow

The bow consists of a 75 cm-long **stick (a)** made out of a fine wood like fir or Pernambuco. The upper end is narrow and sharp so we call it the **tip (c)** or head, while the bottom end is wider and consists of a movable part called the **frog (d)**. All along the stick, between the top and the frog, we can see stretched **hair (b)** made from horse tail. It's important for the hair to be tightened well so we can create the necessary pressure to produce a tone with the string. For that we have a **screw (e)** connected to the special mechanism of the frog which we use to adjust the hair by tightening and loosening it.

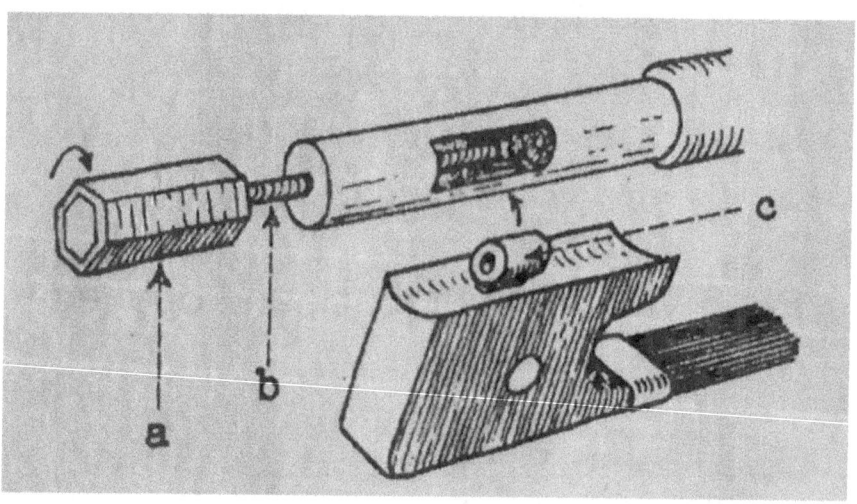

Pic.8 Mechanism of a frog

In the above picture we can see that the screw (a) has its screw bolt which goes through the special ring on the frog (c).

How to prepare your violin for practice

First, we must check if everything is in its place — four tuning pegs and strings, a bridge, four fine tuners, a tailpiece and a chinrest. When everything is checked we can put a **shoulder rest** on our instrument. The shoulder rest is bought separately in any music store or online. We put it on the back of the violin.

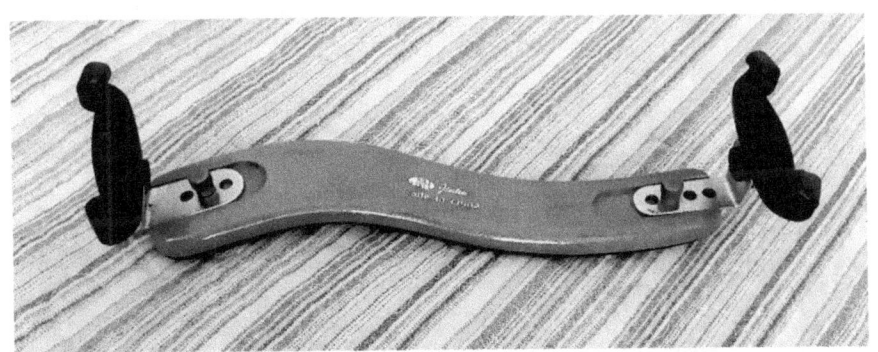

Pic.9 – Shoulder rest

Now we must prepare our bow. We use the screw to make sure the hair is tightened properly. Don't tighten your bow hair too much because it will distort the stick and bounce when you try producing a sound on a string. You can check if you did it correctly by leaning it on the left hand; you will feel if it is tightened more that it should be. Now we come to another additional part we must buy — **rosin**. It is applied along the entire bow hair before every use. Go from the top to the bottom several times and after finishing it, gently swing your bow to remove excess rosin. Now your bow is ready!

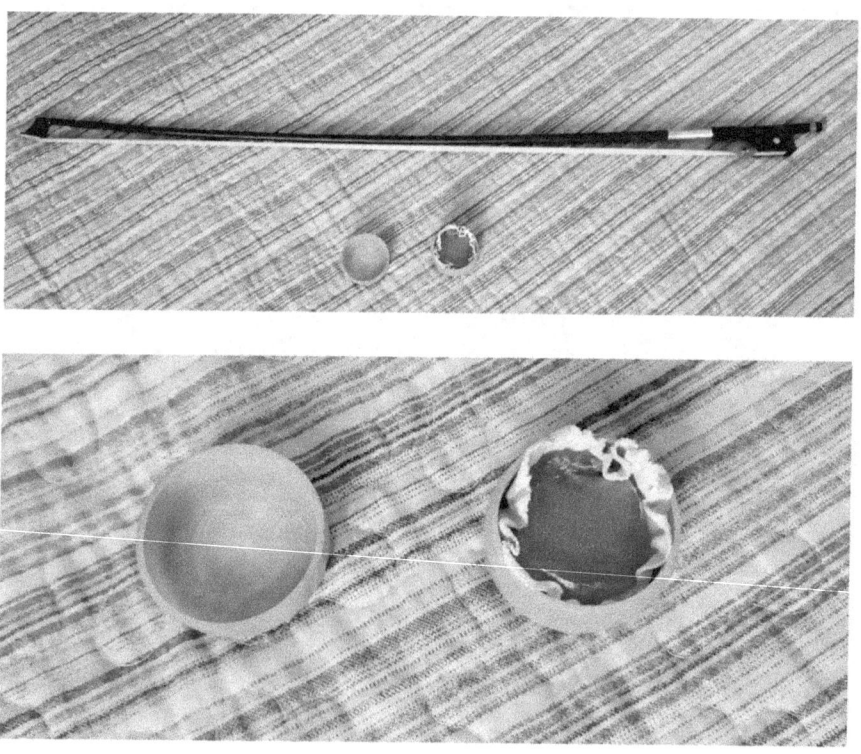

Pic.10 and 11 – Bow and rosin

How sound is produced

In a way, the right hand has a more active role because it produces the sound by moving the bow over the strings. The left hand, however, determines the frequency of the tone because by pressing the string it determines the pitch.

So, we hold the bow with the right hand where the frog is (this will be thoroughly explained in the section about proper posture and how to hold the bow), and we pull it up and down alternately, that is from the frog to the top (a) (this will be marked with the sign Π) or from the top to the frog (marked with V). The pressure is naturally more powerful near the frog than near the top.

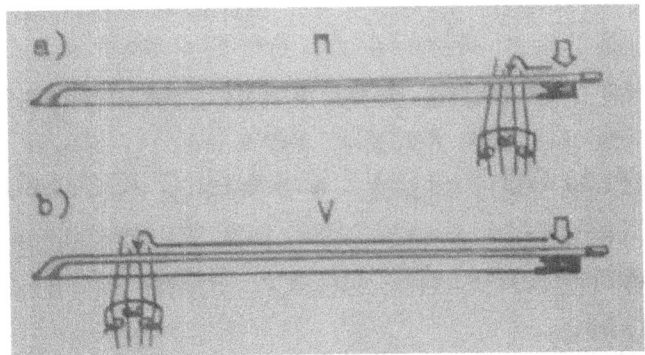

Pic.12 The difference in pressure transfer when the bow is near the frog (a) and near the top (b)

Tuning

The violin has four strings: g, d1, a1, and e2. As we saw previously, each string has its own tuning peg and fine tuner. There are violins that have only one or two fine tuners, on the e2 or the e2 and a1 strings, but it is preferable to buy a violin with four fine tuners. Don't worry; if you already have a violin with only one or two fine tuners, you can add more.

If you want to tune your violin properly, first go to a quiet place. As a beginner, I suggest tuning with an electric tuner. You can buy one in any music store, use an online tuner or download a tuning application on an app store. The tuner tells you whether you are sharp or flat. This is an excellent way to tune your violin while you are still a beginner and you don't have a very good ear yet.

After a while, when you get used to the sound of the violin and the tones we use when tuning, you can try tuning by ear. You listen carefully to the pitch of the note you want to tune (g, d1, a1 or e2) and tune them one by one. You can play your note on a piano, computer or your phone. Always tune string A first because this tone is a concert pitch (chosen standard) to which groups of instruments or music orchestras are tuned for performances.

Whichever way you choose, this is the process: start with the A string, find its peg and turn it to make adjustments. Turn it towards yourself to make the string go lower and away from yourself to make it go higher. Try to match it as closely as possible and then use the fine tuner which will help you find the perfect pitch. Repeat this process for each string.

Basic care

It's important to take care of your instrument if you want it to be with you for a long time. Here are some important things you must pay attention to when taking care of your violin:

- Aside from putting rosin on your bow before every practice or performance, you should also always loosen the bow. Make sure you don't loosen it too much because you do not want hairs to get caught and break. We do this because we don't want to damage the stick of the bow and distort it.

- Always wipe your violin with a soft cloth to remove rosin from the instrument and strings because it can damage them so they won't last as long.

- Keep your instrument in a safe place. Do not keep your violin in extreme cold or hot conditions and always keep it in its case.

Chapter 3

Buying a Violin

Topics covered

- Types and sizes of violins

- Violin features

- Popular brands

- Choosing the right violin for you

The violin is one of the most popular instruments in the world but that doesn't mean it's cheap. Even though the art of making a violin has been studied for centuries, the process of manufacturing one is still complex, so buying a violin that suits you can be challenge. If you decide that this beautiful instrument is going to be your entrance into the world of music, you must be aware of certain things when buying it. This chapter will provide you with all the necessary information for the process of buying your first violin.

Types and sizes of violins

For most of the history of this instrument, there was only one type of violin — acoustic. With advances in electrical instruments, now there is also another type of violin — the electric violin.

The **acoustic violin** is the traditional wooden bowed instrument which produces sound through the connection of the bow and strings which is then magnified by the resonation of the body of the instrument.

The **electric violin** uses the same method of producing sound but the difference is that it uses electrical amplification to send the electronic signal to the speakers or amplification system. Generally, the acoustic violin is better for beginners as the electric violin is considered more difficult to play.

As you have surely noticed before, violin can be played from an early age. When a child gets their first violin, the instrument must be just the right size for them so that the learning process can be as natural as possible. This of course means that the manufacturers have to produce instruments of various sizes to accommodate millions of violinists of different sizes and shapes across the world. For this reason, there are seven main violin sizes you should be aware of before you purchase your first instrument:

1/16: The smallest violin on the market, intended for the smallest pupils. Children age three to five with an arm length between 14 and 15 3/8 inches should use this size.

1/10: This size is suitable for children of the same age with an arm length between 15 3/8 and 17 inches.

1/8: This instrument is for pupils from three to five years old with an arm length of 17.1 to 17.5 inches.

1/4: This instrument is for the next category of children from four to seven years old with an arm length of 17.6 to 20 inches.

1/2: Children from the age of six to ten with an arm length of 20 to 22 inches should use this size violin.

3/4: Almost a full violin, this instrument is most suitable for children nine to eleven years old with an arm length of 22 to 23.5 inches.

4/4: This is commonly known as a full-sized violin and can be played by anyone age nine and above. The shortest arm length a player can have to fully enjoy this instrument is 23.5 inches.

Choosing the right size for your first violin is crucial to your progress and development of the proper technique. Sometimes it is difficult to find the smaller violin sizes, but you would be wise to obtain the perfect instrument for you.

Violin features

Since we're mainly interested in acoustic violins, it should be said that the manufacturing of this instrument has always been considered somewhat of an art form. Every single part of the violin has its purpose and the way it is built will determine the quality of the instrument you are beginning to play. Now we will talk about some features of the violin and how you can recognize a good one from an average or bad one. The most important features fall under three categories: materials, craftsmanship and sound.

Materials

As we have mentioned before, the materials used in the making of any instrument are crucial to their quality. It is no different with the violin. The most important ingredient is, of course, the wood type. Not all parts of the violin are made from the same type of the wood, but there are some combinations of wood that are common. High-quality instruments usually use spruce wood in the manufacturing of the soundboard. Ebony and maple are also good choices as they provide good resonance. The way the wood has been initially treated influences its quality. Of course, it is difficult to detect if the wood used has been dried evenly, but there are some things you can pay attention to in this regard. It is always better to go for solid wood rather than layered materials. If you look closely at a violin you will notice that the back panel is made out of two or more pieces, but this is a common practice and doesn't diminish the quality of the instrument.

Craftsmanship

Although it is an art to make a violin, it should not be an art to detect a good instrument from a bad one. In this section you will learn how. Craftsmen who produce stringed instruments are called Luthiers and as with any other craft, every one of them has their own tricks and theories on how the violin should be made. Of course, handcrafted instruments will always be more expensive than manufactured ones, but in this age of technology, these two worlds are closer than ever. Now there are factory-manufactured instruments that get a crucial personalized touch from a master builder. This is how you can recognize one:

- Hard joints: This is easy to check for and indicates a good instrument. Gently press the body of the instrument and listen for any sounds coming from the violin. There shouldn't be any.

- Scrollwork: The deeper the impression of the scroll detail, the better.

- Geometry: Sometimes it's best to rely on your sight. Look at the violin from as many angles as possible and check if the instrument is symmetrical as it should be.

- The bridge: Although it's one of the most common parts of the violin when it comes to replacement, if you're buying a new instrument, you should check the bridge. Make sure that the bridge is not ill fitted. This is a common problem which usually causes other problems with the instrument.

- Gaps: Be sure to check for any gaps on the violin. They can sometimes be found around the pegs as a result of the instrument not being used in a while. The parts you should focus on the most are around the neck and the box.

- Perfling: The perfling represents the decoration of the instrument along the edge. You should always check if the decoration is even and nicely done to be sure you're looking at a quality product.

Sound

No two violins sound the same. As said before, all the features of the violin are responsible for the overall sound. Even the instruments that have come from the same workshop or factory can't sound the same. Also, it should be noted that some older instruments can be in bad shape which can result in a bad sound. In these cases, it is advisable to consult an experienced craftsman who will tell you whether the instrument can be brought back to its former glory. There is no better advice than to try out as many violins as possible and consult with someone who has more experience.

Popular brands

There are three categories of violin brands: student, intermediate and professional. As their names suggest, and their prices confirm, there are big differences between these categories. Generally, student violins range from $100 to $400, intermediate from $400 to $1,000 and if you decide you want the best of the best and buy a professional instrument you will have to spend at least $4,000 up to millions of dollars for unique antique violins. Since this book is for beginners, in this chapter we'll mention five of the best student and intermediate violin brands in today's market:

Stentor: No list of student violin brands is complete without Stentor. This company produces well-built instruments in both the student and intermediate categories. The prices start as low as $150 so this is a nice starting point for any beginner. The model to look for is Stenton Student I Violin.

Knilling: This company is a bit more expensive than Stentor, but their products offer something special. All Knilling violins are equipped with special perfection pegs which provide much more precise tuning than the regular pegs. If you choose this brand, you will need a budget of around $500.

Cremona: Pricewise, these violins are situated somewhere between the first two brands; you can purchase a nice Cremona for around $300. The company is known for its well-built instruments and prides itself in quality bows. You will be guaranteed their standard level of quality since they have an elite quality control team. The model to look for is Cremona SV-175 Violin.

Cecilio: This company has been approved by violin teachers around the world for years. You might be pleasantly surprised to find out that all Cecilio violins come from the factory with the bridge attached so there's no need for additional assembly. These instruments are mostly made from maple, spruce and ebony and they start at around $200. The model to look for is Cecilio CVN-300 Violin.

Mendini: These violins are in the same price range as the previous ones, so you'll need a budget of around $200. Their biggest advantage is their durability, which is always a big plus when it comes to instruments for children. However, users have in the past found that the factory strings that come with them are of a poorer quality. The model to look for is Mendini MV300 Violin.

Choosing the right violin for you

As you can see, there are many different options when buying your first violin. But don't let this discourage you; you're starting a beautiful journey. There are just a couple more things you should remember before your quest.

You should always try the instrument you intend to buy. If you think you don't have the knowledge needed for this, make sure you have your professor or someone you trust with you when you go shopping. Also, as we mentioned earlier, not every factory violin is the same, so picking a good one can be a challenge even when choosing from the same model. As always with buying, patience is key.

One more option is buying a violin online. This can be tempting because internet shops often provide lucrative discounts, but be cautious. You should always have the opportunity to try the instrument before purchasing it. Here are some things you should consider when buying a violin:

- **What is your price range?** As said before, new factory violins are sold for as little as $100 so you don't have to spend too much if you're just getting into playing. There is also the option of buying a used violin; of course, this requires much more knowledge and experience, so be careful. Since this book is made with beginners in mind, a budget of $500 should be more than enough.

- **What brand falls within your price range?** There are a lot of manufacturers out there so don't get confused. Try to narrow your search down to those which you can afford and avoid the others. Don't hesitate to ask the dealers as many questions as you want to get all the information you need.

- **How long are you planning to play the violin?** This question might seem pointless to someone who is just beginning to take interest in an instrument, but it's worth thinking about. If you consider music a casual hobby, you shouldn't invest heavily in your first instrument. If it becomes more important to you, you can always buy a more expensive instrument later. On the other hand, if you're seriously thinking about a career in music, you should ask your professor for help and purchase an instrument that will help you grow and improve.

Chapter 4

Understanding Music Notes and Rhythm

Topics covered:

- Understanding the staff

- Reading note names

- Flats and sharps

- Counting basic rhythms

Now we can finally start to learn about music. Before you take your bow and make your strings produce a sound you have to understand some basics of music. We will learn here what the staff is, how to name notes, which clef we use for violin sheet, how many keys there are, and some basic rhythms and measures. You are basically about to learn a new language.

Understanding the staff

All music can be written on a staff which you can see in the picture below:

Pic. 13 – Staff and Clef

Every staff consists of five lines and four spaces and each line and space can be a place for a note.

THE STAFF

Lines 3

Spaces

Pic.14

We can also add additional lines above and below the staff:

Pic.15

Although there are different kinds of music clefs, all the music composed for violin is written in **treble clef,** so we are going to learn all the notes according to this.

Pic.16

Perhaps you noticed the vertical lines on our staff. These are called **bar lines**. They appear at the end of every measure like punctuation in a sentence; their part is to visually and logically arrange our music language. Now let's learn how to read notes!

Reading notes

Everything that is written for the violin sounds as it is written. The first thing the professor teaches you is where can you find your four basic strings in a clef. In the picture below you can see our four strings. You can see that the first note **(G)** is written below two extra lines; this is the lowest (in pitch) string. The next one is called **D** (or d1). Then we have **A** (a1) and the highest string, **E** (e2).

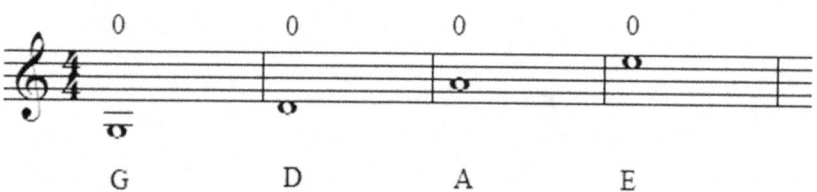

Pic.17

You are probably asking yourself why there is a zero above each note. That's because if you do not use any finger on your left hand to produce the sound, then you are playing an empty string, so we will always mark it with "0," as zero fingers are used.

Now we are going to learn the names of the other notes:

Pic.18

34

You can see in the above picture that some of the notes repeat themselves. There are seven different notes in our system (g, a, b, c, d, e, and f) and they always repeat in the same circle, meaning that when you finish with f, you have a new circle that begins again with g. If this sounds confusing, don't worry. When we start to learn about fingering the strings, everything will become clearer. These are just some small inputs of basics of music theory that are good to know before we start to read the notes and play!

Accidentals

The most used names of accidentals are **flats** and **sharps**. These are the symbols that sometimes appear right before a note. We use them to indicate if we want our note to be one half step higher or lower in pitch. Every note we have learned can be lowered or raised by one half step if there is a symbol to indicate that. If we want to lower our tone, we put "b" after the note (example: B will be Bb). If we want to raise our tone, we put "#" after it (example: F will be F#). In notation these two symbols (b and #) will appear before the notes.

B Bb   F F#

Pic. 19

When we do not want our note to be flat or sharp anymore we can use a symbol which reverses the meaning of these, called a **natural**:

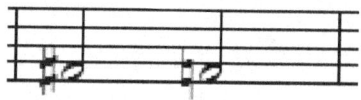

Pic. 20

Counting basic rhythms

Here we will learn the basic rhythms and measures we need to know before starting to read and play the notes. You have probably noticed the different types of notation we used to explain empty strings, notes or accidentals; now we will clarify what these notes are. In the example below we can see different types of notation. We will start from the beginning. The first one is called the whole note and, as in mathematics, everything else is logical. One whole note = 2 half notes = 4 quarter notes = 8 eighth notes = 16 sixteenth notes.

Whole Note Half Notes Quarter Notes Eight Notes   Sixteenth Notes

Pic.21 – Duration of notes

Now we can learn some basic types of time signature. If you remember bar lines from the previous chapter, you know that we use them to separate measures. At the beginning of every staff we must decide in which time signature the composition will be. Here are the most common time signatures:

Pic. 22

Here the upper 4 stands for number of beats per measure and the lower 4 determines the type of note that gets the beat:

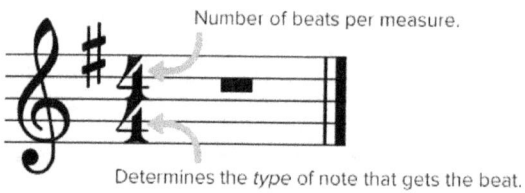

Pic. 23

These are the three most common types of time signatures:

Pic.23 – Time signatures

The first two examples have 4 as a beat but different numbers of beats (2 and 3). The third one has a half note as a beat and 2 as number of beats.

There is one more important part of music that we must be aware of — silence. Silence is an indispensable part of music and in notation it is written with a rest symbol. Rests can have the same durations as notes, but will be written differently.

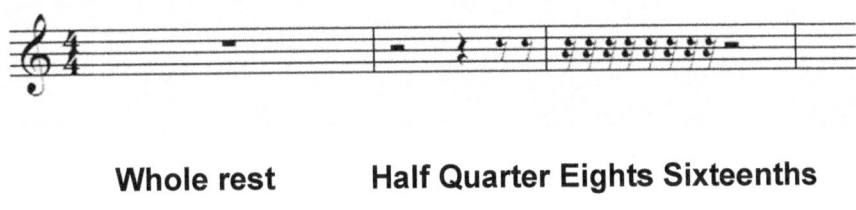

Whole rest　　　　**Half Quarter Eights Sixteenths**

Pic.24

As you can see the whole rest and the half rest are visually the same but the place where you write them is crucial. The whole stands right under the fourth line, while the half rest stands right above the third. The fourth rest is visually different from all the others, while the 16ths are doubled 8ths.

Chapter 5

How to Play Notes: Basic Chords and Scales

Topics Covered:

- Proper posture and how to hold your violin – warm-ups for posture and right hand

- Notes and basic fingerings on the violin – warm-ups for left hand

- Scale studies

- Articulation

Finally! You are about to start applying everything we've learned until now and more. Here we will discuss the best position for playing in, fingerings, and basic exercises, and we will learn more about major and minor scales so that you can read your first composition. At the end we will mention articulation which you will use when playing.

Proper posture and how to hold your violin

It is crucial to learn the proper posture for practice and playing and to apply it from the beginning because it will ensure that you play better in the future. There are two ways of playing the violin: standing and sitting. Maybe you have already noticed that all the soloists play their violin standing (except in cases where they are unable to stand) and in orchestra they play while sitting. It is always better to stand if you can. The first thing you want to do is achieve balance by standing on both of your feet evenly. It is natural to shift your weight, especially after some time, to one side, but it is important to try to maintain balance. It helps to not put your feet too close; you can see this in the picture.

It is also important to stand straight. Your shoulders should be relaxed but level and your knees should be relaxed. If you do need to sit, it is important that you choose a chair with a firm base, sit at the edge of your chair and sit up straight. You can also place your left foot slightly forward for better balance. Now we need to learn how to hold the violin!

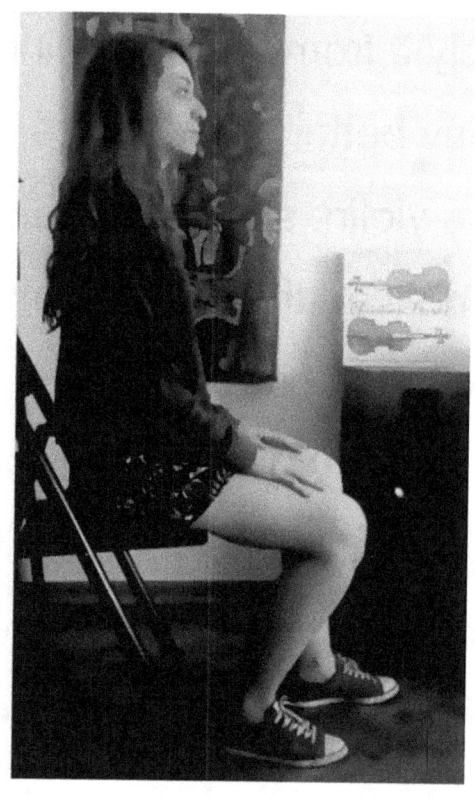

Pic.25

Take your violin in your left hand by the neck and put it on your left collar bone. You can see that the shoulder rest is designed for that so it will lie right where it should. Place the left side of your jaw on the chin rest. The violin should be parallel with the ground and held a little bit to the left (not straight in front you). If you did everything correctly you should be able to hold your violin without hands (try this very carefully).

Now it is time to set the left hand. Hold the neck of the violin between your thumb on one side and your four fingers on the other side. Keep your wrist gently rounded and do not rest your wrist against the neck. Now try to place your first finger on a string to feel how much pressure you'll need to press the string to the neck. Try to practice fine pressure by dropping your finger on the string and immediately lifting it up.

Left hand proper posture

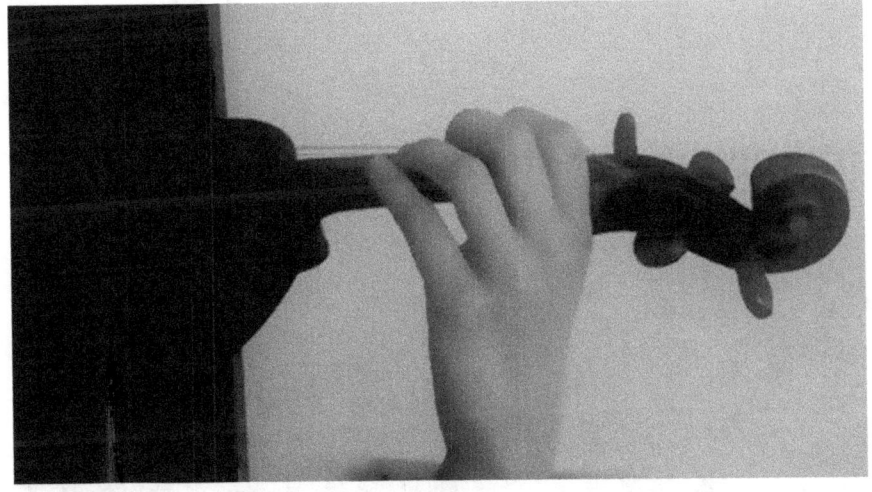

Pic.26

Left hand improper posture

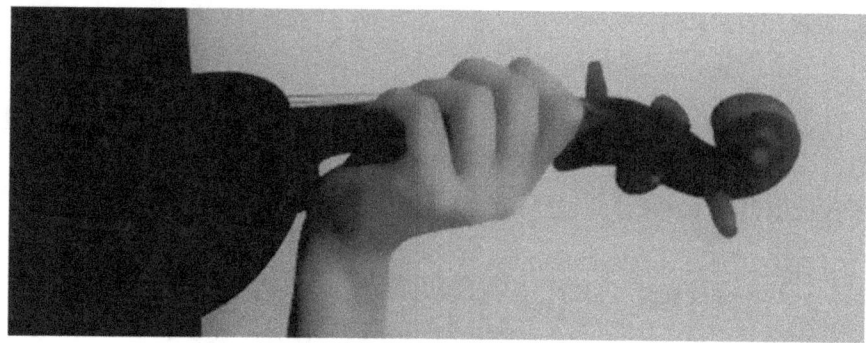

Pic.27

Now for the final touch — adding the bow. Take the bow in your left hand by the stick somewhere in the middle and put your right hand loosely where the frog is so that the stick is right under the phalanxes. Then put your thumb right on the beginning of the frog (in between the stick and hair).

Right hand proper posture

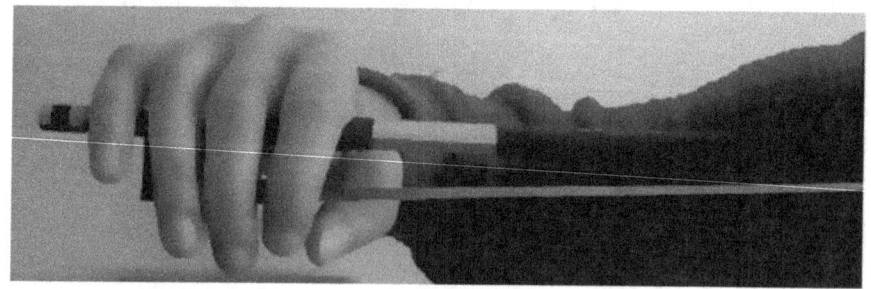

Pic.28

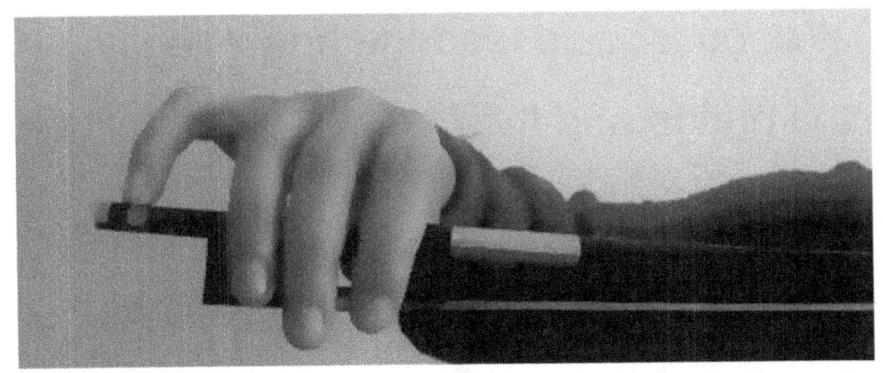

Pic.29

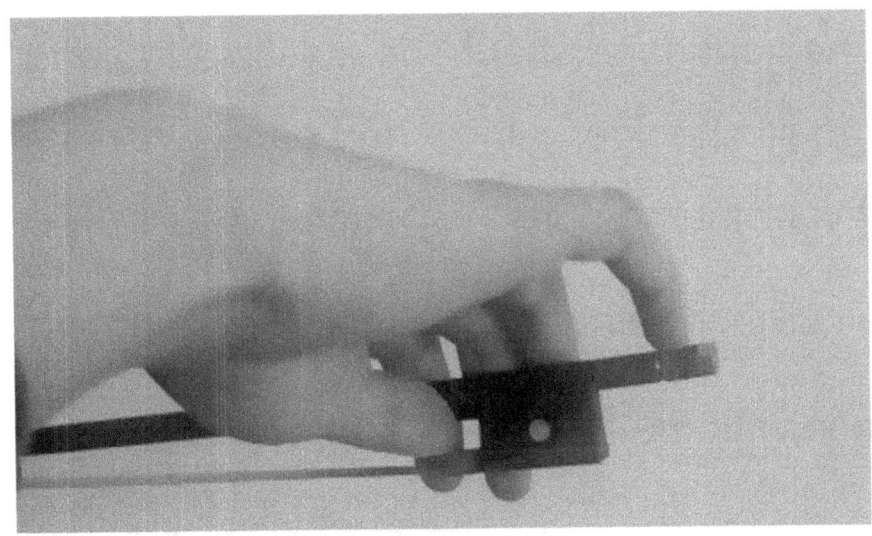

Pic.30

Now put these two together, with the violin in the left hand and the bow in the right hand and slowly lean the bow down to an empty string (choose d1 or a1). The bow should be led throughout all its length, from the frog to the top and the top to the frog. The right hand should not be stiff as a stick but should lead the bow exactly parallel between the bridge and the beginning of the fingerboard.

Now we are going to do a few exercises for empty strings, just to get used to the bow movement. Everything is in 4/4 measure, so we will always count 1+2+3+4 (the first two exercises will have numbers for every movement we make). The right hand should be elastic and bend naturally in all shoulder, elbow and hand wrists and make sure that your thumb does not touch the hair.

Exercise number 1 should be played three times:

- First time with the middle third of the bow

- Second time with the upper third of the bow

- Third time with the lower (frog) third of the bow

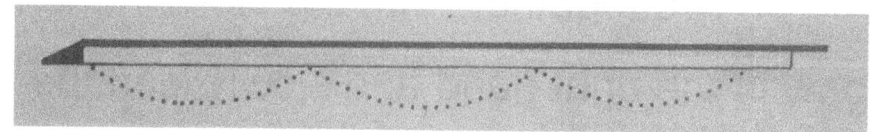

Upper third Middle third Lower (frog) third

Pic.31

Each exercise will be repeated on each of the four strings. When you have rests and no notes to play, do not lift your bow from the string, just let it lie down the string without producing any sound. If you do not remember, we will repeat what these signs mean. When you see "П" you should move your bow from the frog to the top; when you see "V" you should move your bow from the top to the frog.

Exercise 1

1   2   3   4

Listening Example: Exercise 1

48

Exercise 2

We will repeat this exercise twice – first on the upper half of our bow and then on the lower (frog) part of our bow.

Pic.32

Exercise 3

This will be repeated twice – first from the top to the frog and then from the frog to the top.

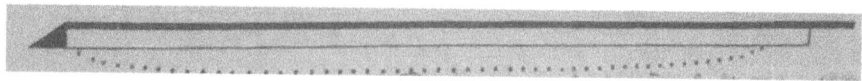

Pic.33

The two vertical lines with two dots is the repetition sign. Everything that is written up until these two lines with dots should be repeated, so every exercise should be played twice.

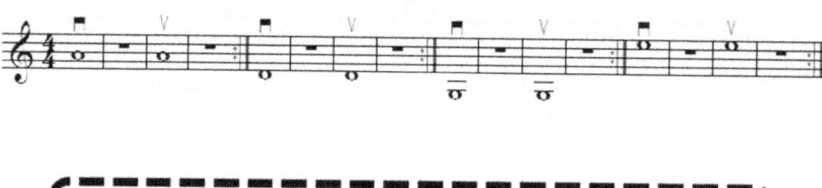

Listening Example: Exercise 3

50

Exercise 4

In the following exercise, when changing the movement of the bow, do not stop its movement. Try to produce as similar a movement as possible for each quarter you play. We will repeat each string three times – on the upper, middle and lower (frog) part of the bow, as we did in the first exercise.

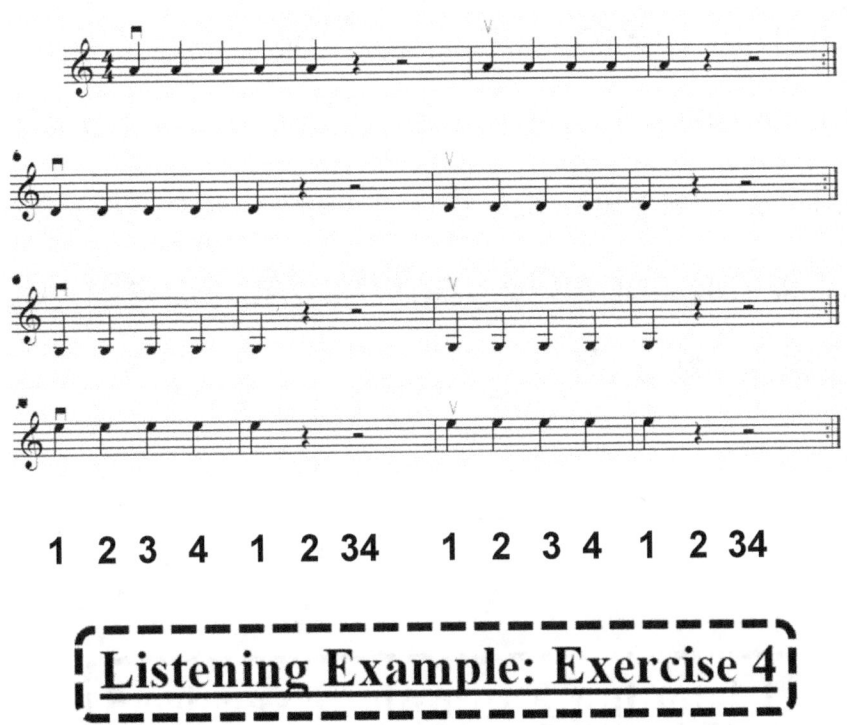

1 2 3 4   1 2 34   1 2 3 4   1 2 34

Listening Example: Exercise 4

Exercise 5

This exercise will teach us how to cross with the bow from one string to another. Do not tighten your right hand when crossing to another string and try to hold the bow as naturally as possible with rounded fingers.

Pay attention to the movement of the bow. When you finish the movement that is signed with V, and after that you do not have a symbol, that means that the next movement is the opposite from the movement you last played (in this case Π).

Listening Example: Exercise 5

Exercise 6

We are going to learn one more thing before we try to put the fingers of the left hand on strings. We are going to learn how to play two strings at once! When doing so the bow should push both strings with the same strength. Here are several variations of the same exercise for two strings:

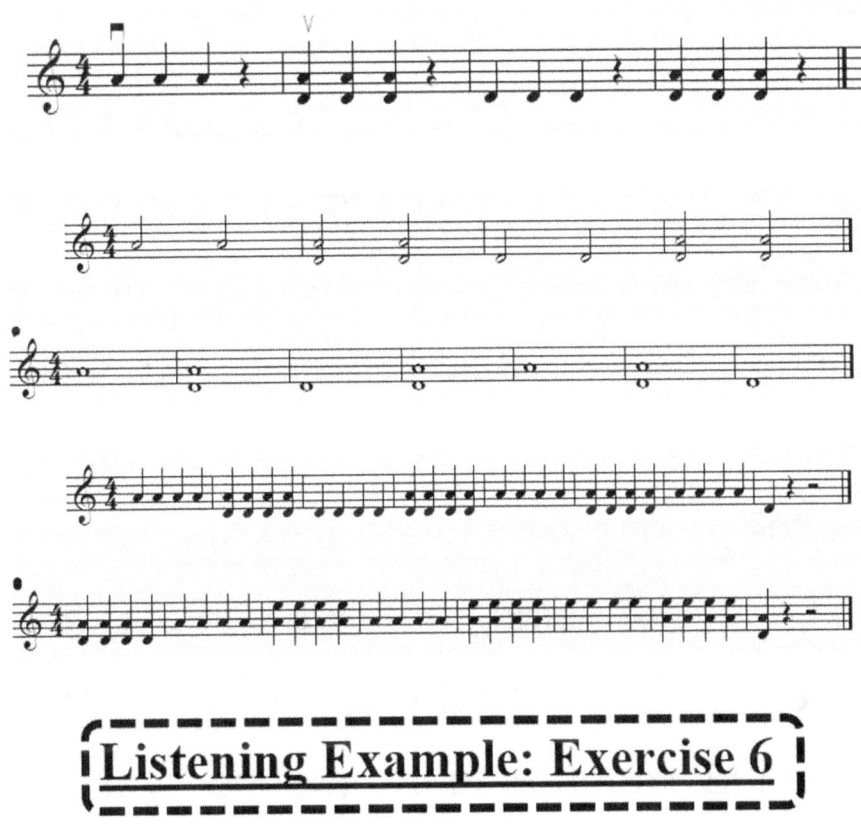

Listening Example: Exercise 6

Notes and basic fingerings: warm-ups for the left hand

The time has come to develop a foundation for the first compositions we are going to learn. We have learned how to properly stand or sit if needed when we practice, how to hold our instrument and bow, and how to use both hands through a number of exercises to which you can always return.

Before we start it is important that you know how to put your fingers on the string. You should press the string with the middles of your fingertips and try not to touch another string. The finger will be slightly inclined towards the nut. Please try this first exercise, which will go through all the strings without the bow. Just put your fingers on the desired string and you can play the sound with the forefinger of your right hand (just to hear it). After you finish all the exercises in this manner, you can take the bow and try them with both hands. If you put your third finger on the string, the first two fingers should stay on the strings; do not lift them in the air!

In this first exercise you will see some sharp (#) tones. That is because we want finger arrangement on every string, for this first exercise, to be the same:

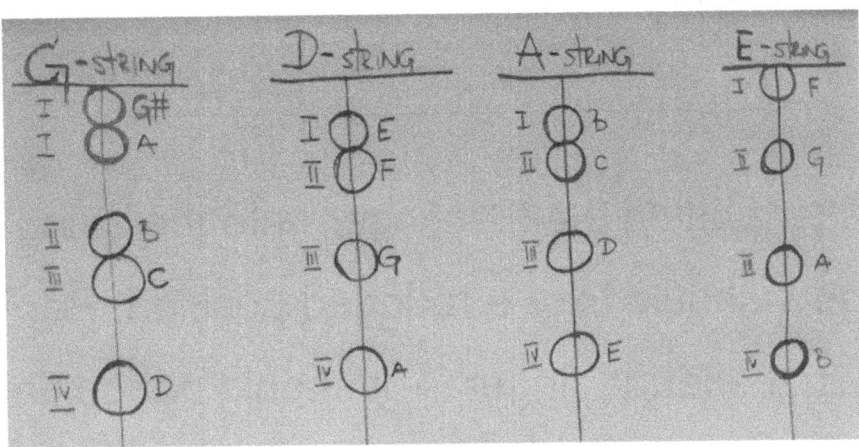

Pic.34

Exercise 7

Advice: after putting the first finger onto the string all the other fingers should take a rounded position. Pay extra attention to the fourth finger — it should not be flat, but rounded like the rest of the fingers.

For the next three exercises play with your bow. **Fingers put and get them off during the rests.** Do not pull your bow off during the rests; it should always be on the string.

Listening Example: Exercise 7

Exercise 8

Exercise 9

This exercise is shown on string D, but after finishing it, you should play it on all the strings (A, G and E).

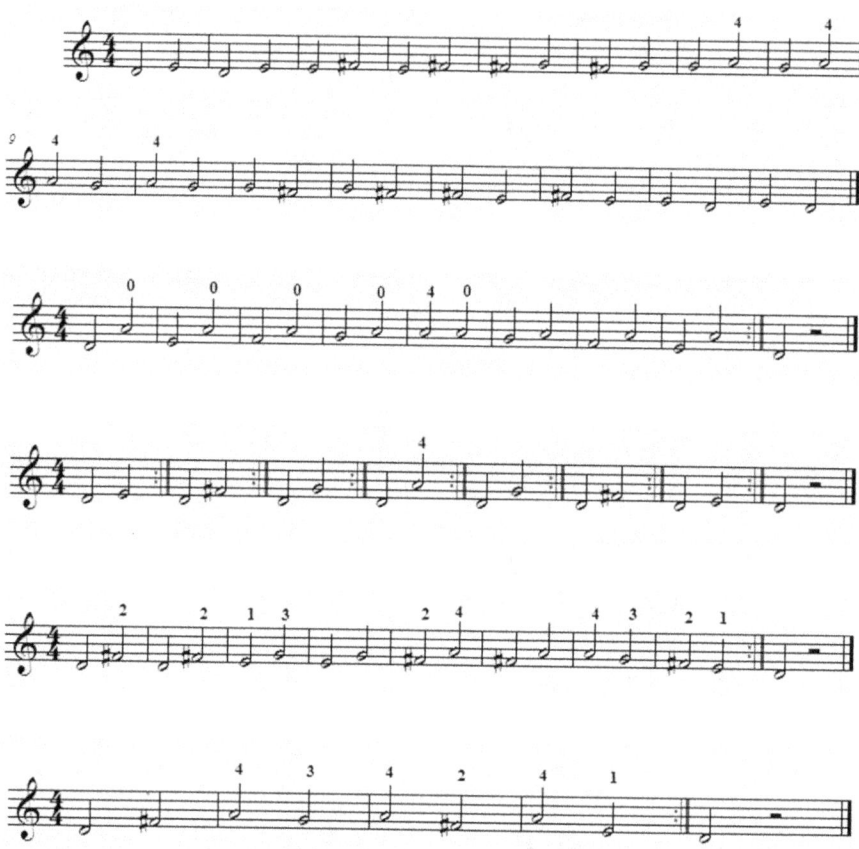

Scale studies

All music is written in one of two keys: **major** and **minor**. We have already been introduced to accidentals (b and #) and we know that when they appear before a certain note they can sharpen or lower its pitch. Most of the time they will be written right after the clef (there can be one or even seven #'s or b's), so you don't have to write it every time you use that note. Why is that? Because it wouldn't be very interesting if all songs were written in the same key.

Before we find out how many keys there are, we are going to clarify what the major and minor keys are. Try to imagine "happy" songs that you know. All of them are written in major scale. What is major scale?

C Major

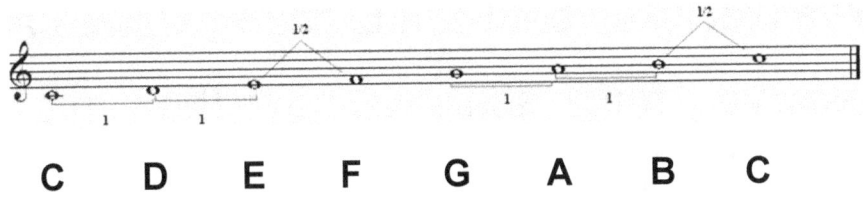

Every scale has eight tones (seven plus the eighth which is a repeat of the first one). These tones have a certain distance between them (some are closer than the others), and every major scale always has the same disposition of tones. As we can see in the example above, the first two tones are a whole tone away from each other, as are the second and third tones, but the third and fourth tones are only four semitones away from each other. This will be clearer if we demonstrate it on piano keys:

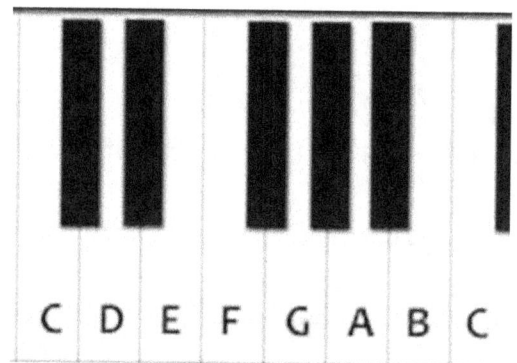

C and D tones have one black key between them. The same thing goes for D and E tones. But as you can see there isn't a black key between E and F, so we call these semitones. Every major scale will have the same disposition of tones and semitones: 1, 1, 1 ½, (1), 1, 1, 1 ½.

Now, try to imagine "sad" songs you know. These are written in the minor scale. The minor scale is a little different because it has three variations. In the example below you will see the three variants of the minor scale.

A Minor – natural

A Minor – harmonic

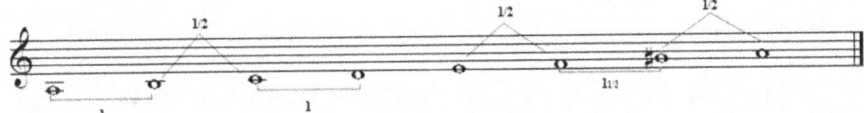

A Minor – melodic

Notice that the disposition of the first four tones is always the same because that is the pillar of the minor scale when the other four tones can change their space between them. The second – the harmonic scale – has its seventh sharpened and the third one – the melodic scale – has its sixth and seventh sharpened. It is pretty clear from this why the first one is called natural.

After defining the major and minor scales we come to the final step: learning how many major and minor scales there are. We always begin with **C major** and **A minor** because they do not have one sharp or flat note (or if you look at the piano keyboard, they are played only on white keys). One major scale always has its minor pair (with the same number of #'s or b's). The picture above lists all the major and minor keys with their parallels. We have seven sharps and seven flats – the same number of accidentals as the number of notes! So everything is connected. At some point you will learn all the scales, but until then you can always refer to this list and check which scale the composition you want to play is in.

Now we will go through some exercises that include some of the mentioned scales. Always remember the first finger arrangement we learned (where we put the first, second, third and fourth fingers on every string) and when we have # on the place of the finger we didn't have before, that is the time we move that finger a little bit more towards us! If, on the other hand, we have b (flat) in front of the note that we didn't have before, we must move that finger slightly away from ourselves. Keeping that in mind, let us go through several exercises in different keys.

Exercise 10

D major, A major, G major and E major (notice the number of sharps after the clef and pay attention to the fingering).

1

2

3

4

At the end of this section it is important to mention **intervals** — the distance between two neighboring tones. There are: unison, second, third, fourth, fifth, sixth, seventh and octave (that is the same tone we began with, but for the octave up or down). What follows are exercises for each of the mentioned intervals:

Exercise 11 - intervals

Second (2)

Third (3)

Fourth (4)

Fifth (5)

Sixth (6)

Seventh (7)

Eight (8)

Articulation

While the left hand is responsible for the pitch of tones you play, the right hand is responsible for the manner of the notes you play. Basically, bow movement can be divided into three groups: lying moves (we do not lift the bow from the string while doing these types of movements), jumping moves (more or less bow jumps on the string) and thrown moves (we practically throw the bow to the string and it bounces off and returns).

Lying moves

Détaché: every tone is played separately (as we did until now).

F. Mendelssohn - Midsummer night's dream, overture

To this point we played every note we had separately, but there is a way to play several notes through the same move of the bow. This is called **legato** and in the sheets it will be represented with a convex line connecting two notes we want to be played on the same bow movement (or if you have, for example, five notes you want to play on the same bow movement, you will connect the first and fifth note with the beginning and the end of the curved line).

You can also see the > symbol, which adds accent to the note, so this note is more emphasized than others. Martellato movements are short and brisk – hammer like. It is mostly used when you are meant to play louder.

L. v. Beethoven: VIII Symphony, F Major,

op. 93, 2nd movement

Jumping moves

The most well-known jumping move is spiccato, where the bow lightly and, if needed, with high speed bounces off the string, usually on the middle.

L. v. Beethoven – VIII Symphony, F Major, op.93, 2nd movement

Staccato is a difficult bow movement. Certain bigger lines of short-sounded tones are played through one-direction bow movement.

H. Wieniawski – II violin concerto, D minor, op. 22

Throwing moves

The border between jumping and throwing movements is not very clear but there is one typical thrown movement – Jeté-ricochet. It is played in such a way that the bow thrown onto the string is bounced and comes back three to four times.

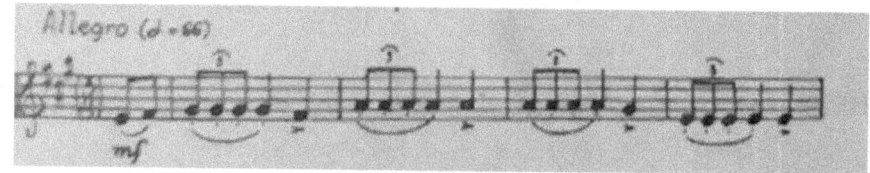

N. Rimsky-Korsakov – Spanish capriccio

There are other bow movements which do not belong to one of these three groups that we mentioned.

Portamento is sort of an aggravated legato, where we underline every played note within joint bow.

A. Borodin – II string quartet, D Major – Nocturne

Tremolo is a special kind of articulation. You make very fast and short movements, in both directions, to create continuous repetition of a tone. There are two kinds of tremolo: tremolo staccato and the **real** tremolo.

L. v. Beethoven – IX Symphony, D Minor, op. 125, 1st movement

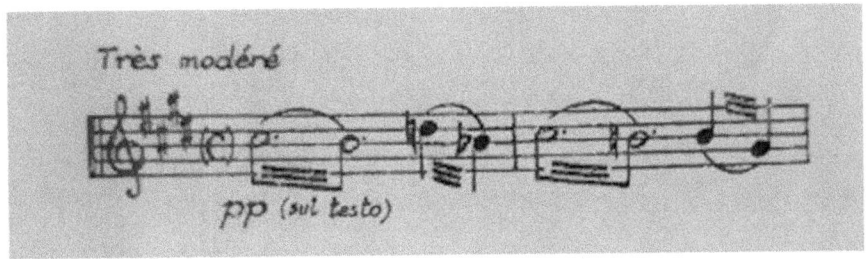

B. Debussy - Afternoon of a faun

This last movement we will mention is rarely used. It is called con legno. For this movement we do not use the hair to produce the sound but the stick of the bow itself. These movements are mostly short, jumping moves.

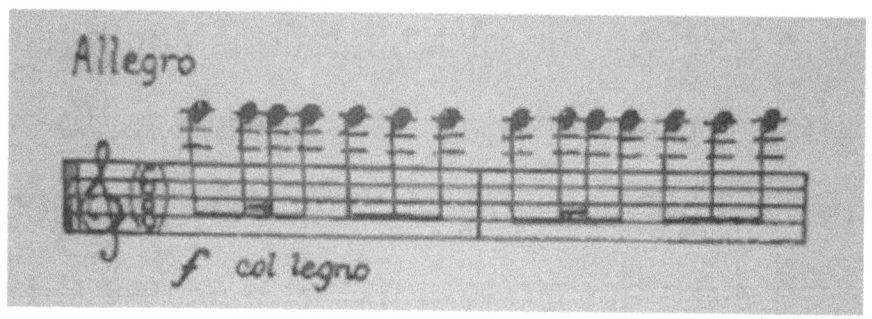

H. Berlioz - Fantastic symphony, 5ft movement

We have added some extra exercises before we play some popular and known songs.

Exercise 12

Exercise 13

Exercise 14

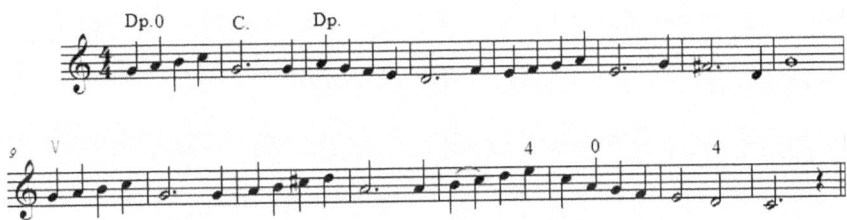

Exercise 15

Exercise 16

Exercise 17

Etude- Marjanovic

Chapter 6

Examples of Songs to Play

After spending some time playing the exercises and scales we prepared for you, it is time to go further and play some songs! We have selected some standard learning songs for you, but after that the possibilities are limitless. It's time to play some music!

Twinkle, Twinkle Little Star

┌───┐
│ **Listening Example: 1. Twinkle, Twinkle, Little Star** │
└───┘

Mary Had a Little Lamb

Folk song

Listening Example: 2. Mary Had a Little Lamb

Song

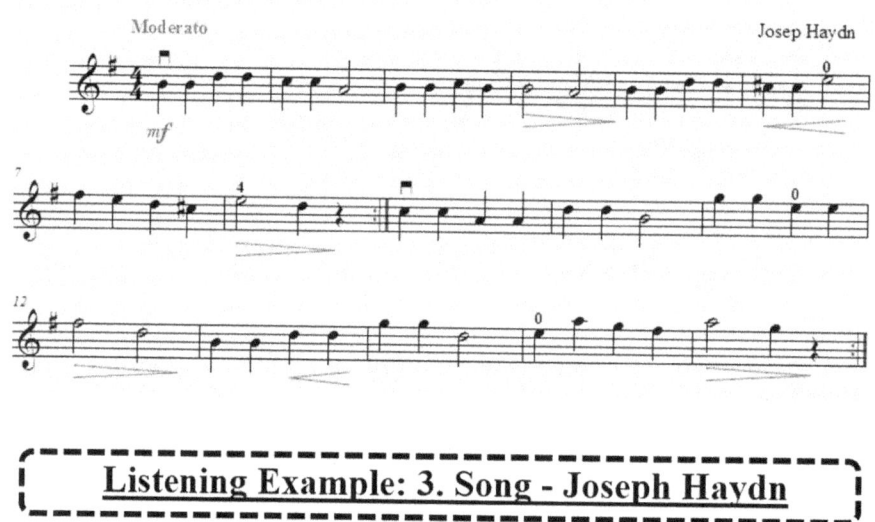

Moderato

Josep Haydn

Listening Example: 3. Song - Joseph Haydn

Ode to Joy

March

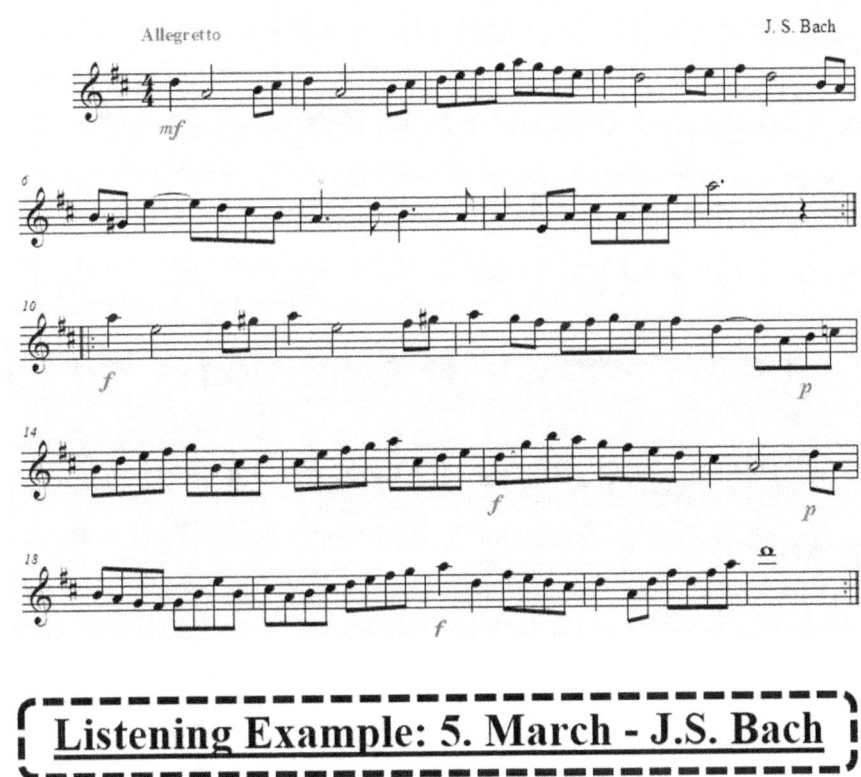

Chapter 7

Conclusion: Bringing It All Together

Everything you have read and learned here is valuable, whether you decide to play for yourself at home, or for your friends and family, or you want to share your music with others through a band. Whichever you choose this will change your perspective of listening and understanding the world of music. This wonderful skill will be part of you for the rest of your life!

If you wish to expand your knowledge and technique, we have selected some pages that can help you find more music sheets and everything else we have mentioned in this book – metronomes, tuners and honest advice.

Here are some suggestions on where to find more sheet music for violin:

- https://www.8notes.com/violin/sheet_music/?difficulty=1

- https://violinsheetmusic.org/

- https://www.musicnotes.com/sheet-music/instrument/strings/violin-family/violin/style/pop

- https://www.virtualsheetmusic.com/violin/

Here are some online tuners for violin:

- https://www.violinonline.com/tuning.html

- http://www.get-tuned.com/html5-violin-tuner.php

Here are some online metronomes you can use:

- https://www.metronomeonline.com/

- https://www.8notes.com/metronome/

- https://www.imusic-school.com/en/tools/online-metronome/

Unlock Your Musical Potential:

Get 30% Off the Next Step in Your Instrumental Journey

As a token of appreciation for your dedication, we're excited to offer you an **exclusive 30% discount** on your next product when you sign up below with your email address.

Visit the link below:

https://bit.ly/40NikR2

OR

Use the QR Code:

Unlocking your musical potential is easier with ongoing guidance and support. Join our community of passionate musicians to elevate your skills and stay updated with the latest tips and tricks.

By signing up, you'll also receive our periodic newsletter with additional insights and resources to enhance your musical journey.

Your privacy is important to us. We won't spam you, and you can unsubscribe anytime.

Don't miss out on this opportunity to continue your musical journey with this special discount. Sign up now, and let's embark on this musical adventure together! 🎼